Fun with I

Fun with Digital Photography

Written by John Larish

Publication AC-260
CAT No. E129 1147
Library of Congress Catalog Card Number 96-70653
ISBN 0-87985-786-2
Printed in the United States of America
Design: Andrea Zocchi Design

KODAK Books are published under
license from Eastman Kodak Company by
Silver Pixel Press®
21 Jet View Drive
Rochester, NY 14624
Fax: (716) 328-5078

Fun with Digital Photography

by John Larish

Table of Contents

1 Why Digital?

A high-resolution digital image can be virtually indistinguishable from a photograph taken conventionally on film.

If you're not a computer whiz or an electronics junkie, your first question upon opening this book is probably, "What can digital photography do for me?" The answer is, an enormous amount, with ever-expanding applications for both your personal and professional life.

Don't Have a Computer?

At its most basic level, you don't even need a computer or digital camera to participate in digital imaging. Any function described in this book can be performed by a service provider, so long as you know what to ask for and are willing to pay the price.

You can have conventional photographs (prints, negatives, or slides) scanned by a photofinishing lab, copy center, or service bureau. Using those vendors that offer self-service kiosks, you can add text and graphics to photos to make personalized greeting cards, calendars, or other creative items.

A very popular service offered by many photofinishers is to digitally reproduce prints for which you've lost (or never had) the negative. This service can be taken one step further—many of these same labs can retouch damaged prints and make copies that look like new. This is an especially popular way of restoring antique pictures that might have been damaged over the years.

Select the best photos from your family album and have them written to a CD.

You can view your photographs on your TV by having them written onto a KODAK PHOTO CD Disc and playing them on a KODAK PHOTO CD Player—a great way for the whole family or a group of people to view your "family album" at once.

If you're thinking about investing in a computer, go for a test drive first. Have a few images scanned onto a floppy disk, and ask a friend or relative who has a computer if he or she will help you experiment. Once you see what can be done with images on the computer, I will virtually guarantee that a computer will top your gift wish list!

ONCE YOU HAVE A COMPUTER

To select a computer that's right for your digital photography needs, first shop around, asking as many people as many questions as you can think of. Then, armed with recommendations, choose an appropriate software application. Read the packaging to find the list of memory requirements and other specifications required for the application to be run effectively (see Chapter 3 for more on computers).

Once you have a computer and imaging software, the door is open to countless artistic, professional, and just plain fun possibilities. To whet your appetite, I'll touch briefly on a few of them here, and more thorough explanations will follow in upcoming chapters. All of these possibilities require digitizing an image, which is explained in Chapter 4.

Photo Screen Savers

I've found that immediate digital gratification can be achieved by making your own computer screen savers. If you leave your computer on for a long time without using it, the image on the screen will be "burned in." A screen saver protects computer monitors from this problem. Screen-saver software automatically switches from the document or image on your screen to a moving or constantly changing image after a set amount of time has elapsed or upon command. With simple software you can replace a ho-hum stock screen saver with a rotating album of your personal pictures! Take a phone call or a coffee break and return to find a picture of your kids smiling back at you!

Make your own postcards to send to friends and family.

Personal Correspondence

At home you can dress up your letters with photographs, design family newsletters, produce decorative "to do" lists, or create original greeting cards or postcards with photographs, text, and other artwork.

The Professional Edge

Whether you work at home or in an office, full-time or part-time, being able to use digital imagery will give you a professional edge. It's been proven that people respond better to documents that include photographs. You can vastly improve the impact of something that's as mundane as a memo or as important as a presentation. Even if you never plan on touching a computer, just knowing what can be done will allow you to conceptualize projects such as these and delegate the work to qualified personnel or vendors.

Starting Young

It's not hard to see that this is the dawn of the digital age, and the worlds of education and business have been forever changed by the computer. Give your kids a head start by introducing them early to computers and digital imagery. The more comfortable they are on the computer, the better equipped they'll be for the challenges that lie ahead. Even youngsters who can not yet read can have wonderful fun with the software art programs designed for kids.

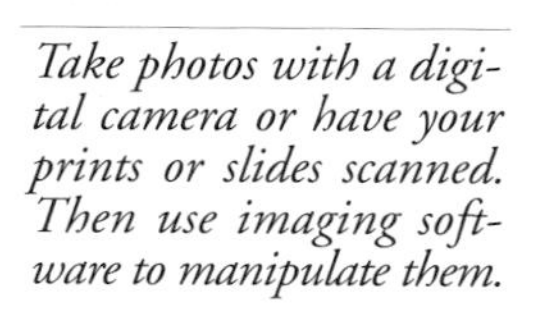

Take photos with a digital camera or have your prints or slides scanned. Then use imaging software to manipulate them.

Pursuing Artistic Endeavors

Computer software lets you easily alter, manipulate, paint over, or combine photographs. Almost everyone can enjoy this new art form, and it doesn't require years of art classes. It's easy, fun, and almost addictive!

THE INTERNET

And let's not forget the phenomenon of the Internet. Those who are hooked in know how much fun it is to share information, e-mail, and pictures with virtually anyone else who has Internet access. The Internet can be described as a giant invisible web connecting people and businesses who have a computer and modem. Originally developed decades ago as a way for scientists to share information, the Internet has now taken on a life of its own.

For those who have not yet been initiated, the "Net" may seem an intimidating concept—but it's not intimidating in reality. The best way to get your feet wet is to visit a friend who is on the Internet and take a tour with him or her. Then visit a computer store to find out what you need (a modem, for instance) and how to hook it up. Online services such as America Online® and CompuServe® often offer free introductory subscriptions and software, so you can see if you like the world of the Internet before you commit yourself financially. Local businesses and phone companies are starting to offer Internet access as well, which will ensure competitively low prices. And keep an eye on your local cable TV company, since Internet access through your TV is about to hit the mainstream.

Online services offer the option of attaching a file, such as a digital picture, to an e-mail message. This is a quick, easy, and inexpensive way to share photos with family and friends.

Self-serve photo kiosks or imaging stations let you scan a print or slide, crop it as desired, and print out as many copies as you need.

Surfing the Net and the Web

The first thing most people use on the Internet is e-mail. Instead of making phone calls, sending faxes, or using overnight couriers, you can transfer text, pictures, and virtually any digital file electronically via e-mail.

In addition, you can join live "chat forums" with people all over the world and talk with them as fast as you can type. Games of chess or

Through the Internet you can visit various "web sites" and see everything from a florist's offerings...

...to the sights of other countries.

backgammon can be played at any time of day with people anywhere in the world. The Net also offers free computer games and software that can be downloaded onto your computer.

Beyond that, there's the joy of "surfing the Net" to look for specific information and entertainment, or simply to browse. The Internet itself has unwritten rules that "require" it to be a tool for research and the sharing of information. However, a branch called the World Wide Web, or "Web" for short, is designed to be the commercial sector of the Internet. Companies (or private individuals) can create "web sites" or "home pages" that can be visited by people who access their "addresses." One web page can be linked to another, allowing viewers to go from window to window, somewhat like turning the page in a catalog. Or they can have "gateways" and "hot links" that automatically link you with other related Web addresses.

Even the commercially oriented World Wide Web usually heralds back to the altruistic goals of the Internet, with the most successful web pages offering the lucky visitor information or entertainment. For example, a bookstore's marketing strategy might be to lure you to its web site with lively book reviews of trendy new novels or an interview with a best-selling author, hoping you will linger long enough to purchase books from them.

Lists of interesting and informative web sites can be found in the slew of new Internet magazines, newspaper columns devoted to the subject, or directories sold in bookstores.

Now, let's get to work!

Creating Your First Digital Photo

2

Whether you're new to photography or have been taking pictures for years, digital photography offers a variety of new creative opportunities. Digital imagery in its simplest form allows you to view your snapshots (saved on computer disk or KODAK PHOTO CD Disc) on a television or computer screen, or you can send them out for others to see via the Internet. You can have quality prints made from the digital photo files at photo labs, camera stores, or even at home. Or you can use self-service kiosks (or software on your home computer) to make greeting cards, montage prints, newsletters, and much more.

Digital Cameras

It's easy to get started in digital photography because there are so many ways to approach it. The easiest, albeit most costly, method is to begin electronically by shooting a picture with a digital camera. These cameras work similarly to conventional cameras—except they record the image on digital media instead of on film.

And, as with conventional film cameras, there are different types of products to choose from to meet different needs. Every digital camera has a limit as to the information (or resolution) that it can record. Be aware, though, that resolution is closely linked to the price point of the camera.

Software for your home computer lets you turn photos into creative greeting cards.

If you don't have immediate access to a computer, you'll want to use a digital camera that stores images on removeable PC cards.

Selecting a Digital Camera

Low-resolution, entry-level digital cameras can be compared to basic point-and-shoot cameras. They typically have fixed-focus lenses (non-autofocusing) and limited picture-taking capabilities with no advanced functions. Digital cameras usually save the pictures internally (usually up to 16 or 32 images). The camera is then connected to the computer with a cable, and pictures are downloaded straight onto the computer's hard drive. Some cameras allow you to view your images on TV by plugging the camera into the TV's video input socket via a cable.

Point-and-shoot digital cameras are a great choice for taking snapshots and for general photography, as well as commercial applications like shooting pictures for the company newsletter or real estate listings. The down side is that once you shoot your limit of "keepers," you need access to a computer in order to download them.

Higher-end digital cameras solve this problem by allowing you to save the pictures to PCMCIA (Personal Computer Memory Card International Association) cards (we will call them PC cards for short). These cards can then be removed and transferred to the computer via a special card reader. If you're traveling or are away from your computer (or your laptop is too heavy to carry), you can bring along extra PC cards like extra rolls of film.

At the top of the list are high-end professional digital cameras that cost tens of thousands of dollars. It is these expensive models that supply pictures to newspapers around the world within minutes of an important event's occurrence or are used in the studio by commercial digital photographers.

Don't think using a digital camera will limit your subject matter. Even low-light situations and fast-moving subjects don't pose a problem!

When pricing digital cameras, keep in mind that over the years you'll be saving a lot of money in film and processing costs. In the world of digital photography, you can "erase" a picture and take a new one over it once you've transferred the image to a computer or disk or decided it's not a "keeper."

Take a digital snapshot from the television screen or videotape.

Digital and Video

There are products on the market that let you "grab" still images from a videotape. You can use this technology to go back through your video collection and save digital snapshots. You can also use these products to capture images off of a television or video-game screen.

YOU DON'T NEED A CAMERA

There is no rule that says your digital image has to start with a digital camera. You can have film negatives, prints, and drawings digitized and placed onto a disk for you to use.

There are many options for home scanning, including scanners designed for standard 4 x 6-inch photographic prints. There are also high-end models that are capable of producing high-resolution images suitable for framing or professional use. Some scanners can scan film, some can scan photos and other flat artwork, and some can do both. And all of these scanners can be linked directly to your computer via cables and allow you to easily save the newly digitized pictures on your hard drive.

If you don't want to invest the money or space on your desk for a scanner, don't worry. Most quality photofinishing labs and many copy centers offer scanning services for very reasonable prices. In addition, computer specialty services and mail-order businesses are starting to appear all over the

Having your favorite photos scanned allows you to crop, colorize, and otherwise manipulate them on your computer.

country offering both input (scanning) and output (printing) services. For the sake of simplicity, I'll call all these sources of inputting and outputting "service bureaus." These companies will scan the picture at whatever resolution you require and deliver it on floppy disk, KODAK PHOTO CD Disc, or other digital data storage system (such as Syquest® cartridges or Zip™ disks).

If you just want to get your feet wet and "test" some of the ideas laid out in the following chapters, using a service bureau is a good way to get started. When you're sure you're "hooked," you may want to consider investing in your own scanner (see Chapter 4).

What Is a Service Bureau?

Service bureaus are businesses that provide digital imaging services, such as printing from digital files and image scanning. They may also offer computerized retouching, restoration, and graphic design. A service bureau could be considered a digital photo lab and in fact, many photo labs have expanded to include imaging services.

What Kind of Computer Can I Use? 3

As you become more involved in digital photography, you won't always want to rely on a service bureau for all your digital imaging needs. Having a computer with graphics capabilities offers greater creative control and allows you to explore new techniques. Both PCs (IBM and IBM-compatibles) and Macs (Apple Macintosh® and Mac-compatibles) can be used in digital imaging.

Once you load the image into the computer, several factors will affect the computer's ease of operation and the image quality.

How powerful your computer needs to be depends on how much you want to manipulate your photographs.

What's Under the Hood?

The power of your computer's "engine" will affect the quality of the image you will be working with (ranging from low-resolution black and white to high-resolution color) and how fast the computer performs the tasks you ask of it. It's no fun sitting at your desk, tapping your fingers, watching an image come up on the screen a millimeter at a time.

Your computer's ability to process images depends on four factors: the Central Processing Unit (CPU), the Random Access Memory (RAM), Bit Depth, and the monitor itself. For all these factors, more is better—but "better" is a relative term based on your needs, goals, and budget. A city snow plow might be the best in the world, but do you need that much power if you're just clearing your driveway? Check the list of requirements on the software packaging to make sure that your computer has what it takes to run the application effectively.

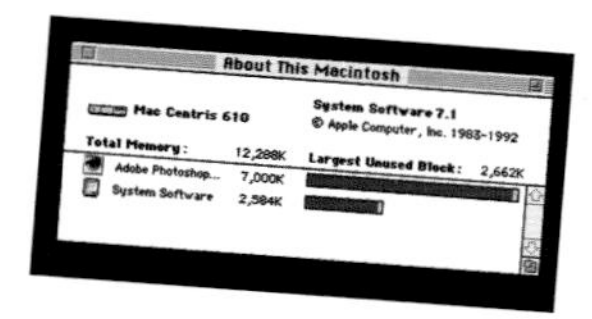

Photo manipulation programs need a lot of RAM to process images. Your computer must have the minimum amount of memory required by the software.

CPU Power

The CPU is the brain of the computer, so the bigger and stronger your CPU is, the better. Almost any computer sold today will have enough power to run simple images. If you're planning to do high-end graphics and desktop publishing, you probably won't be happy with the lower-end choices.

RAM and VRAM

If the CPU is the brain, then RAM is the short-term memory that lets you hold an image on screen and work with it. Four megabytes (MB) of RAM is the bare minimum for the simplest imaging applications, and most photo-manipulation software requires at least 8 MB of RAM. The good news is that RAM is expandable on most computers. So keep expansion potential in mind when you're purchasing a computer. Some computers require Video Random Access Memory (VRAM) as well for top-quality image display on the monitor. These are separate memory chips devoted to image display, affecting the resolution and number of shades and colors you see on the monitor.

Binary Digit (Bit) Depth

Binary Digit or Bit Depth determines the quality of your photograph—it is roughly equivalent to "grain" in conventional photography. A computer and monitor with 1-bit capability can deliver only

These images approximate how a photograph will appear on a monitor at various bit depths

black-and-white images. Don't confuse this with a black-and-white photograph, which has many variations of gray in it. One-bit color produces only black and white (in other words, monochromatic or line art). Four-bit capability lets you use 16 levels of gray or color, which still looks fairly primitive. But if you're new to digital imaging, watching these images come up on your computer will still feel like magic.

For accurate color rendition, your monitor should be adjusted to match your printer. Otherwise, the image might look great on the screen but not when it's printed out.

Eight-bit capability provides 256 shades of color. Although that may sound like a lot of shades, images viewed on an 8-bit system don't look as seamless as a color photograph. However, if you're just planning on doing black-and-white work or simple home projects with digital imaging, this amount of bit depth is more than adequate.

Sixteen bits expand the system's capability exponentially to 32,000 different colors, making the photograph look pretty good to everyone but an expert. At 24 bits and 32 bits, there are 16.7 million colors to choose from—which approximates photographic color. If you're planning on doing professional or commercial applications that require photographic quality, complex image manipulation, or slick reproduction in magazines, books, or advertisements, you'll need at least 16-bit, but preferably 24-bit, capability.

THE MONITOR

The monitor on your computer has enormous influence on your ability to work with digital photos. A black-and-white monitor is never going to show your image in color no matter how big a computer you attach it to. Likewise, for high-level color work, you should be able to adjust the color balance of your monitor so you can evaluate and correct color casts and shades.

Using your computer and a modem you can instantly send and receive photos of everything from your new grandson to roses in a gardening catalog.

MODEMS

Modems are basically telephones for the computer. By attaching the computer to a modem, and the modem to a standard phone jack, your computer can talk to other computers or join the biggest party line of all, the Internet. This means that you can send files from one computer to another using your home telephone or any phone, including cellular and airplane phones! (Why drive to work?) You can even create a gorgeous full-color document on your computer monitor, then send it via the modem to a service bureau that can print it out for you.

Both picture and text files can be sent via modem. But because of the huge amount of information contained in picture files, you'll want a high-speed modem to keep your phone time down. You are billed for the time that is spent on the phone line.

Faxing via Modem

Incredibly enough, modems with built-in fax capability (some are available now for less than $50) can turn your computer into a fax machine that's capable of receiving and sending faxes (so long as the document you are sending is in your computer). This lets you fax your digital images without ever investing in (or finding a space on your desk for) a conventional fax machine.

Environmentally sensitive individuals will love the fact that they can view the faxes they receive on the computer screen, save them to computer files, erase them, or forward them to another party without ever wasting a piece of paper.

The Ins and Outs 4

Chapter 2 touched briefly upon methods of getting the images into your computer. Here those methods are covered in more detail, with an explanation of how to get your images out of your computer when you want to share them.

A photofinisher or service bureau can scan your photos or slides and give them to you on a floppy disk or CD.

Yawn, Yawn, Yawn...

If computer tech stuff bores you to tears, you'll be glad to know you can skip this chapter and just use service vendors to digitize your images and later print them out as the need arises. Camera stores, photofinishing minilabs, copy shops, or a new breed of business called a "service bureau" all offer these services.

But if you're intrigued by the creative potential of digital photography, you may want to consider the options discussed here and in the next chapter.

Inputting Images

Creating a Digitized Image

There are two ways to create a digital photograph: You can scan an existing image (such as a conventional photograph), or you can shoot an image with a digital camera. Scanning an existing photo can be done by a service bureau, such as a photofinisher, copy shop, or computer specialty service center. The service bureau will deliver the digitized image to you on a floppy disk or KODAK PHOTO CD Disc. If you own a picture scanner, you can scan the image yourself and

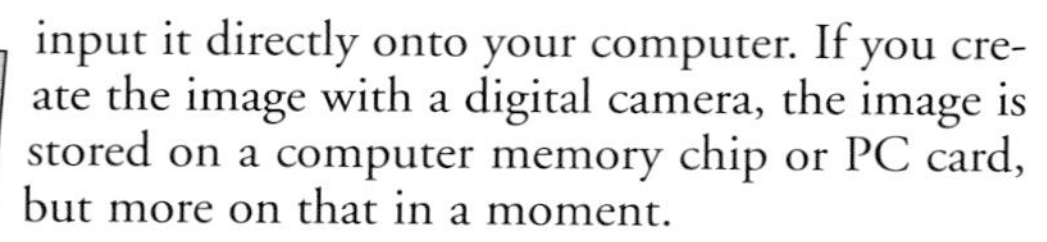

input it directly onto your computer. If you create the image with a digital camera, the image is stored on a computer memory chip or PC card, but more on that in a moment.

Experiment! Instead of flat art, these translucent glass beads were placed on the flatbed of a print scanner.

Scanners

Today easy-to-use compact desktop picture scanners allow you to convert existing color or black-and-white pictures to digital data in your home. There are different types of scanners that can scan prints, flat art, or slides.

These scanners connect easily to computers and usually come complete with all the software you need to convert your pictures into digital information. Often the scanners provide other functions such as cropping and adjusting the color balance through their software programs (see Chapter 5).

The price of your scanner goes up with the level of resolution it is capable of producing. If your scanner's resolution is low, you will be able to see the individual pixels that make up the picture (called pixilation), and the picture will look fuzzy. The larger you print the picture, or the closer you are to the picture when viewing it, the more of a problem this becomes. If it looks too fuzzy, try scanning it at a higher resolution, or try printing it at a smaller size.

You can scan a photo at low or high resolution, depending on its purpose. When image quality is not important, low resolution is used to keep file sizes small. In order to hold image detail, a high-resolution scan is required.

Digital Cameras

Similar to a computer's hard drive, a digital camera's internal computer chip has finite memory capacity for storing image data. When this memory chip is full, no more pictures can be taken without first downloading them onto a computer or inserting a PC card (a replaceable memory source) if your camera can accept it. PC cards allow you to change "film" by switching cards when the camera's internal memory or the memory in the currently loaded card is full.

Digital cameras are made to download images from the camera's internal memory or a PC card directly onto a computer. Most digital cameras can be plugged into the computer as if they were auxiliary hard drives or other peripheral device. Images stored on PC cards can also be downloaded by using an accessory PC card reader, freeing you up to continue shooting with the camera.

Images taken with a digital camera are downloaded directly onto a computer. They can then be combined with text and printed.

OUTPUTTING IMAGES

Print Size

Most images made by simple digital cameras are best printed to a maximum size of 4 x 6 inches. On occasion an image of outstanding quality can be printed in a larger size, but that would be an exception. If the scanner is capable of very high resolution, photographs from conventional cameras can be printed to 8 x 10 inches or larger, including poster-sized prints.

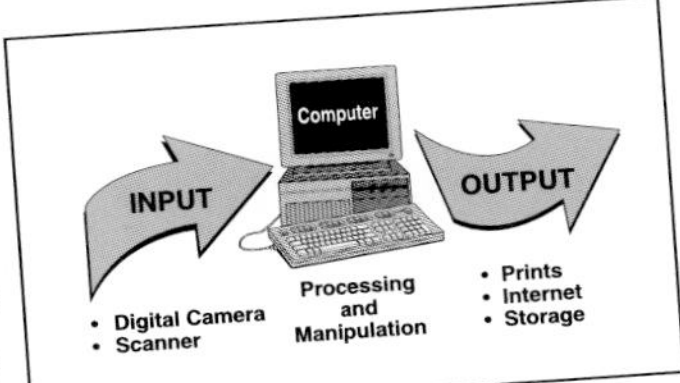

The Digital Camera: How It Works

In a traditional camera, film is the recording medium. In a digital camera, the charge-coupled device (CCD) is the film equivalent. Both film and the CCD record pictures, but at that point the comparison stops.

CCDs have a two-dimensional array of points on which the entire picture can be captured with one exposure. CCD sensors are monochrome devices but can record colors through the use of color filters—similar in concept to the different dye layers on color films.

Imaging with a CCD is performed in three steps. First, exposure to light is converted into an electrical charge at individual points (pixels) on the sensor. Second, these charges are transferred by moving packets of the charge within the silicon photo diode. Third, the charge is changed to a voltage and then output.

Printing Your Pictures

Great strides have been made in digital printing capabilities since the medium was first introduced. There are now many options on the market, ranging widely in price and picture quality. Don't make your purchasing decisions based on digital pictures you saw a few years ago (or even a few months ago!).

Whether you choose to purchase a home printer or use a minilab or service bureau to print for you, you'll be pleasantly surprised at what you can do with digital photographs from digital cameras or pictures converted from film-based photographs.

For printing good-quality digital pictures, there are several excellent choices, including ink jet, thermal, and other printers that utilize silver-halide process products (conventional photographic papers). All of these types of printers produce digital pictures with photo-like qualities both in resolution and color saturation. Here again, the better the quality, the higher the price—whether you're buying the machine or just paying a minilab, quick print lab, or other vendor to make the print.

Adding a printer to your computer setup allows you to output your photos to share with family and friends!

Home Sweet Home

Today a number of printers are available that can make good-quality color pictures at home from your digital files. The quality of home color printers has improved dramatically, at almost the same rate that their prices have dropped. It's a win-win situation for the digital enthusiast.

There are three common types of color printers for home use. Thermal and ink jet printers are not new but have been greatly refined in quality and are now very reasonably priced. Color laser printers are more costly and only recently have become economical enough to be considered "home" units.

Ink Jet Printers

Because significant progress has been made in the design of ink jet printers, many newer ones can output at nearly photographic quality. This is particularly true if the picture can be printed on high-quality paper and at resolutions of 600 dots per inch (dpi) or greater. "Photo-look" papers are available with a smooth surface. Unfortunately, many of the inks for ink jet printers are water-soluble, and other printing methods should be chosen if the image may come in contact with moisture (unless you intend to laminate it).

Many service bureaus are equipped with color copiers that can output digital files.

Thermal Printers

Thermal printers produce results that come the closest to having the look and feel of traditional color photographs (from negatives). Heat is used to transfer the colors to the paper. Some printers provide a protective finishing layer that is applied after the dyes are transferred. This protective layer reduces fading and prevents fingerprints from affecting the dye in the prints. However, this protective layer is currently available primarily on large-format commercial-quality printers.

DPI and Printing

Digital output devices are measured in the form of dots per inch, or dpi. To maximize the perceived sharpness of a digital picture, the pixel count of the image-capture device must be aligned with the desired output size and the dpi of the intended output device(s). For instance, an image consisting of 600 x 450 pixels will appear perfectly sharp when printed at 2 x 1.5 inches on a 300 dpi printer (2 inches x 300 dpi = 600 pixels, 1.5 inches x 300 dpi = 450 pixels).

The important point is to match the output print size with the resolution of the CCD in the camera. For example, a 2 x 3-inch print coming from a lower-resolution camera (fewer pixels) can look great. If you try and make the same image into a 4 x 6-inch print or larger, you will see some loss of detail.

Laser Printers

Until very recently, few choices were available in color laser printers. Now, lower-priced laser printers with high-output capacity (number of prints per minute) for the desktop are available. The challenge will be to bring the cost down to the level of today's black-and-white laser printers.

SAVING PICTURE FILES

Memory Hogs

Regardless of how you input your pictures, you'll need a good method for saving them. The problem is that picture files tend to be much larger than most text files because they contain so much information. Digital photographs are memory hogs!

I recommend that you save only the pictures you use most often (or those you are currently using) on your hard drive and back these up to another storage medium whenever possible. If you have a hard drive that's small or nearly filled, you could slow down your other functions by loading up the memory with too many photographs. You also risk losing them if you have an irrecoverable hard drive failure. Your "photo album" or library of other photographs should also be stored in this fashion.

One of the nice things about digital filing systems is that mini-print indexes can be printed for easy reference. Some software programs refer to the small pictures as "thumbnails" or icons. When you have conventional film images put onto a KODAK PHOTO CD Disc, the CD comes with these mini reference prints.

To conserve valuable computer memory, don't store photographs on your computer's hard drive.

Backup Systems

The cheapest, easiest, and most universal method of saving digital pictures is to use back-up floppy disks. If you're saving strictly low-resolution or compressed files (see page 25), this is just fine. But when you start getting into bigger and better picture files, you could end up with an image that is too big to fit on a common 3.5-inch floppy disk!

Like the familiar floppy disks, PCMCIA cards are very useful for short-term storage and allow for fast transfer onto your computer. They come in a variety of storage capacities and are capable of being erased and reused. While the cost of the cards is higher, their small size, convenience, and high capacity bring down the cost per picture as you reuse them.

Archive your irreplaceable family photos on a KODAK PHOTO CD Disc.

If you plan to do a lot of work with digital imaging (or want to back up a lot of other files and applications as well), you might consider other storage systems with more memory than floppy disks. Syquest® drives for cartridges with up to 140 times the storage capacity of one double-sided 3.5-inch floppy are commonly used in the graphic arts and business fields. And the more economical Zip™ systems from Iomega are making inroads, especially for home use. To run Syquest cartridges or Zip disks, you'll need to buy the appropriate auxiliary drive.

If your computer has a CD drive, you'll love the KODAK PHOTO CD format. You can have your pictures scanned to a KODAK PHOTO CD Disc by a vendor. (Or buy a CD writer if you're really ambitious!) What you'll get back is a CD that can hold up to 100 pictures, all indexed with mini prints for quick reference. This system makes it really easy to locate the pictures you want.

Keep Organized!

If you hate not being able to find a book on your shelf or in the library stacks, then imagine the frustration of trying to find a certain digital photo in a pile of loose disks! Digital cameras and vendors all tend to code pictures with numbers. Take the time to rename each picture file with a code

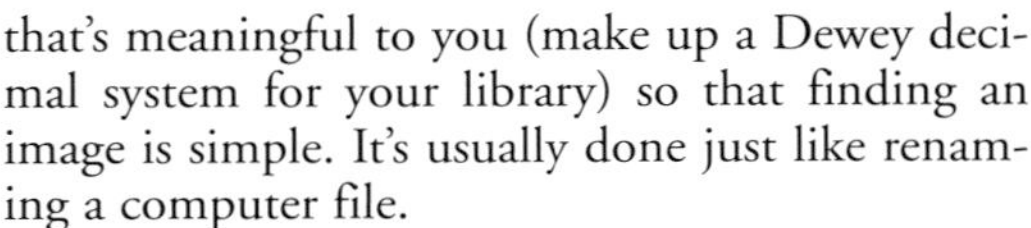

that's meaningful to you (make up a Dewey decimal system for your library) so that finding an image is simple. It's usually done just like renaming a computer file.

For example, when a digital camera is connected to a computer and the pictures are downloaded, each image has usually been given a very basic identifying label. It might be "IMAGE 01.TIF" or a date and frame number. When you bring up a thumbnail picture on the monitor, the image's name will appear underneath. Just click on the name and type in a new name that's easy for you to remember.

Vendor Services

For many people the real fun of digital photography may come in letting someone else do all the work after pressing the shutter release. For others, there is also fun to be had in using the software programs and outputting the image themselves—similar to working in the darkroom.

Before you take your work to a photo dealer, it is important to decide what you want done. This saves time for you and assures that the work you request will meet your expectations. Communication is the most important aspect of getting good work at a reasonable cost with any vendor.

Outside services can be found at self-service kiosks in some shopping malls, photo labs, copy shops, and computer specialty stores. Also, computer magazines list mail-order services if time is not a problem.

My coding system includes the initials of the subject, followed by an abbreviated description or date. "RE95-Xmas" for example, might be a picture of my wife, Rose Ellen, on Christmas Day in 1995. Similarly, "Suns-ESB" is my sunset picture of the Empire State Building in New York City.

You could waste a lot of time wading through disks trying to find a particular image. Make it easy on yourself and give each photo a recognizable name, such as "GoldGateBr-6/95."

If you're saving photos to floppy disk, weigh the cost versus convenience. At under 30¢ apiece (when purchased in quantity or on sale), I think it's worth the money to create a separate disk for each person, holiday, year, event, or type of photograph.

Compression

Compressing files can help you when storing pictures on floppy disks or other media because, as its name suggests, it reduces the file size of the image so that it takes up less space in the computer's memory or on the back-up disk. However, it is important to note that once a picture has been compressed, it cannot be restored exactly to its original form. Compression is one of the things that makes transmitting pictures easier today, by reducing the time required to send them from point to point. The most commonly used compression system is probably JPEG (Joint Photo Expert Group).

You can select the amount of compression used by choosing low compression (which will produce an almost exact copy of your original picture) or high compression (which may lose some information but will speed up the transmission of a picture and make satisfactory pictures for screen-viewing). If you must compress a file, consider the use and choose the amount of compression carefully so that as much information as necessary is retained.

5 Playing with the Software

The City of Köln

by Barry Cohen

Integrate photos into school or business reports for added impact.

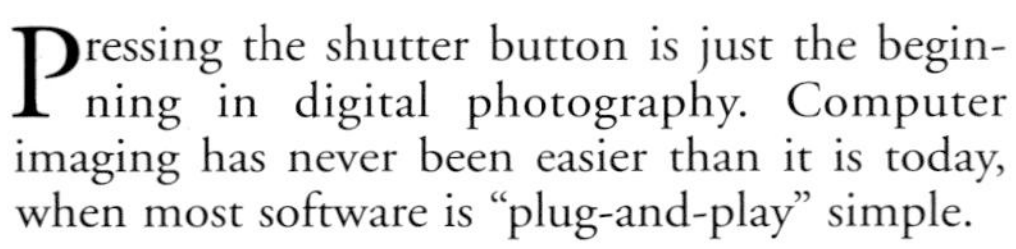

Pressing the shutter button is just the beginning in digital photography. Computer imaging has never been easier than it is today, when most software is "plug-and-play" simple.

Words and Pictures

The easiest way to get started is to use the picture exactly as it comes out of the digital camera, off the scanner, or from the KODAK PHOTO CD Disc and add it to a text document. Most of today's word processing software systems will take digital pictures and integrate them with text. It takes a few minutes to read the instruction manual to learn how to import a picture into a digital text file, but it is worth the effort.

In most cases, the program's menu will give you the option of bringing a graphic into the document. You just indicate where you want the graphics file (picture) to be placed. At that point the words will flow around the picture, and the picture will become an integral part of your page. You can import a picture made by a digital camera directly or use copy-and-paste commands to bring it into the software you are using. Advanced programs let you run text over the pictures or do "magazine-style" graphic effects.

Make your own letterhead using the font of your choice, and personalize it with a photo.

Adding Text

One of the most useful features of digital photo software is that you can add words to a picture file to create posters, greeting cards, certificates, or simply identify the people in the picture. Almost every enhancement program available today has the ability to combine words with pictures. The words can be in a variety of typefaces (fonts), so pick one that suits the mood of the image and is easy to read. If you want to get fancy, you can purchase more fonts or even have one made from your own handwriting.

Add text and make your own holiday greeting cards.

Most programs allow type to be set in a variety of sizes and colors. You can pick colors that blend harmoniously with the picture or pick bold or complementary colors (like blue and orange) for added emphasis.

DIGITAL DARKROOM

If you want to improve or alter your digital image, you can enter the world of the digital darkroom. Instead of being a room full of enlargers, negatives, sinks, and chemicals, today's darkroom is on your desktop in the form of a computer and keyboard. Think of it as a digital imaging center that is fun for the whole family. (See Chapter 7 for lots of fun ideas for integrating digital photography into your family's lifestyle.)

Digital photos can be altered to achieve effects that would be difficult to create with conventional darkroom techniques.

Once an image originating from a negative, print, videotape, or digital camera file has been digitized, you can begin a most exciting and creative adventure. Using any of the hundreds of available photo software programs, you can enhance, correct, modify, or alter your digital picture dramatically.

Even very basic imaging software offers features such as cropping, vignetting, and toning.

These programs range from the very simple to the very sophisticated. They can be acquired free as share-ware from the Internet, or you can purchase programs that range from basic photo-fun packages to professional imaging software that costs hundreds of dollars to buy and takes weeks or months to master.

If you're using a digital camera, it probably came with software that allows you to view your pictures and make some improvements to them. Often scanners come with software that can do many basic photo-enhancement functions.

Simple Programs

The first wave of graphics software programs were aimed at professionals. The programs are complex and require powerful computers to run. Most amateurs do not need these and prefer to start with simple programs. As digital photography becomes more popular, simple and inexpensive programs that include the most useful features are becoming more widely available.

For the average picture-maker, the important thing is that the subject, whether it be a person, place, or thing, is recorded faithfully. The beauty of digital photography is that the picture-maker gets many chances to make improvements.

If you didn't compose the image perfectly in the camera, use your image-enhancement software to crop it or remove distracting elements.

THE UPS AND DOWNS OF CROPPING

With even simple software, you can crop a picture to improve its composition or eliminate unwanted elements. Digital cropping can be compared to taking a 4 x 6-inch print and cutting off some of the edges with scissors—for instance, snipping off an abundance of gray sky on top and some "empty" space to the right and left of your subject. You'd then have a much smaller print (say 2 x 3 inches), which could be enlarged back up to 4 x 6 inches. What you'd end up with is a 4 x 6-inch print in which the subject is more prominent. The same thing can be done in the digital environment, only more quickly and easily.

Unfortunately, it's not a perfect world. If you enlarge a small section of any photograph (conventional or digital), you'll get diminished picture quality. For this reason, it's always better to make your compositional decisions in the viewfinder before you take the picture and rely on cropping only as necessary corrective surgery.

Cropping enables you to improve the composition of a picture and delete unwanted elements to call attention to the subject. But you may lose image quality if you enlarge the cropped portion of the image.

IMPROVING EXPOSURE

One of the first things you may want to try is to improve the exposure or the colors in your digital picture. With some software programs, this may be a simple command that lightens or darkens the entire picture. In others, more elaborate features are offered that allow you to control the shadows (dark areas), middle tones (gray or halfway between light and dark), or highlights (the lightest parts) of your picture. Or you can select and adjust a small area of the photo, such as a person's face. Complex programs let you dodge or burn (lighten or darken) specific areas of a scene, which produces similar results as the traditional darkroom manipulations.

Instant Suntan

With digital pictures from a camera or scan, you have complete control over the color. For example, unflattering skin tones that look greenish in a picture can be corrected, and even a suntan can be added! Or if you want lusher greens in a nature scene, you can simply "turn up the volume" and increase the color saturation.

Selectively touch up the colors in your photograph to make eyes sparkle and cheeks glow.

This sounds easy, but before you know it, a "little change" has gone too far. Instead of giving a suntan, you've given a sunburn! Fortunately, most programs have an "undo" command. That's the beauty of the digital picture. You can always go back to where you started and try again. Some things will not work the way you expect them to. Sometimes there are pleasant surprises in the results you obtain. The fun is in the exploration.

Bad Lighting?

Most digital cameras produce correct color rendition when shot in daylight or with flash. However, if you are shooting a subject lit primarily by fluorescent lighting, the picture will have a green cast, and shooting under standard incandescent bulbs will give the image a warm cast. Correcting color casts is also easy to do. Try the different color-correction options your software offers. Remember, if you are not happy with the color correction, you can return to your original picture by using an "undo" or "revert to saved" type of command.

RESTORATION

It's especially fun to restore old pictures. Either take a copy photo with a digital camera that has close-focusing capabilities or have the original photo scanned. Both will produce a digital file. Once the picture is in a digital form, scratches can be removed, tears repaired, and many other age-incurred problems corrected. Even fading can be corrected through the use of the contrast, brightness, and/or tone controls that are available in many software programs.

RETOUCHING

Paint or airbrushing tools work very well for erasing small skin blemishes or large mistakes like trees growing out of the subject's head. The real trick is to enlarge the picture on the monitor to a size that allows changes to be made gradually. Pick a color reference point that approximates the color you want to use. You will be surprised at how quickly you can produce satisfactory picture corrections.

Make "old-fashioned" photos with your computer. Digitize a photograph and alter the color balance to appear sepia-toned.

EPS, TIFF, JPEG, GIF, Huh? Picking a File Type

Different word processing and graphics programs require that you save your images into different file types, such as EPS, TIFF, GIF, PICT, or other such designations. These formats simply translate the digital information into a language that the software understands. For example, the most popular way to send pictures over the Internet is in GIF format (this compresses the file, making file transfer faster). Hence the Internet slang "send GIF ASAP" means that your correspondent is waiting on the edge of his or her seat to view your image.

Check the instruction manual on your word processing or desktop publishing software to find out what kind of picture file formats you can use.

READY FOR THE TABLOIDS

More sophisticated photo-enhancement software lets you combine two or more images to look like one original. This can be done for aesthetics or for fun. It can be as flattering as replacing a bland background with a pretty sunset or as funny as putting different heads on different bodies for a "tabloid" scandal effect. Crude combinations can be done quickly. High-tech, seamless combinations require top-of-the-line software and hardware and a lot of patience and skill.

MORPHING

Children and adults will enjoy the mind-dazzling effects that can be created by morphing. Hollywood started this trend with movies like "Terminator 2" and "The Mask," which both made use of morphing technology.

A number of software packages are now available that allow you to take a still picture and manipulate individual areas. While most applications can be a source of great fun, they can also be put to more practical use such as trimming wild, fly-away hair. Most morphing programs allow you to take a point in a picture and move it, stretch it, curve it, or alter it in many other ways. A series of individual steps will allow a waistline to be tucked in or expanded, or with a single touch to each corner of a mouth, you can create a smile.

Don't take digital imaging too seriously. Have some fun and try effects that make you laugh!

Artistic Effects

Once you understand the ABCs of handling a picture digitally, you may be itching to go further. Many software programs allow you to take your picture and add "filters" that make it look like an oil painting, watercolor, or line art. You can also choose different paint brushes and colors, and paint over portions of the picture to add color to black-and-white photographs. Or turn modern photos into sepia-toned "heirlooms."

6 Shooting Great Pictures

Whether you take pictures on film or with a digital camera, it's important to hold the camera steady. Keep your elbows in and, if possible, brace yourself against a solid object.

The best way to get good digital pictures is to start by taking good photographs—whether you use a digital, an SLR, or a point-and-shoot camera. This chapter is designed to give you a few pointers that will vastly improve your results. For more information on how to improve your picture-taking skills, check out the many KODAK Books available from Silver Pixel Press.

Steady as She Goes

There are a few basics that will ensure that you get good pictures, no matter what kind of camera you use. Holding the camera in a steady position is one of the first things to concentrate on. Keep your arms close to your sides or, if possible, brace yourself against a building or another solid surface. If you are prone to shaking when you take a picture (or your results are often blurry), try holding your breath for a brief second while you press the shutter button. If you're really serious about your photography, you can purchase a tripod (they come in a wide range of prices).

Most entry-level digital cameras and many point-and-shoot cameras have a slight pause between the time the shutter is pushed and the picture is actually captured. With practice, the difference will not be noticeable unless you are shooting something with a lot of action, like a basketball game or other sports event.

A typical example of "camera shake."

Sharp Pictures

Camera shake isn't the the only cause of unsharp pictures. If the subject is moving too fast for the shutter speed, it will appear as a blur, but the background will be sharp (provided the camera is held steady). Also, the subject must be within the camera's focus range. For autofocus cameras, the focus point must be on the subject.

When made or viewed at low resolution, digital photos may appear unsharp or have image defects, such as aliasing or moiré.

Picture Quality

It is important to understand what elements make up picture quality. When we look at a picture, we consciously or subconsciously look for three things:

1. PICTURE CLARITY Is the picture clear? Does the subject appear sharp and in focus? Are edges well defined?

2. DETAIL Can we see detail in the dark and light portions of the picture? For example, can we see the detail in a person's hair? This is called "dynamic range." With digital imaging this is primarily a function of the number of discrete "steps" that the camera's sensor and signal processing are capable of delivering.

3. COLOR Are the colors accurate? Do the grass, sky, and skin tones all look real? Color perception and evaluation are very subjective, yet certain elements act as color references in any picture we make.

There is one additional factor to digital image quality:

4. IMPURITIES Did the digital process accidentally cause distortion or lines to appear that were not present in the original scene? Is there aliasing (jagged lines or edges) or moiré (an undesirable pattern, most often found when the subject has repeating patterns in it, like a checkered tablecloth or striped shirt)? Is there color fringing or bleeding, especially in high-contrast portions of the image?

Check your camera's minimum focusing distance. If you're too close, the photograph will be out of focus.

That's Close Enough!

Many of the simple point-and-shoot cameras have a *minimum focusing distance.* This means they can not take sharp pictures of anything that is closer than this distance to the camera. If your subject is closer than the camera's given minimum focusing distance, the picture will appear out of focus. Check your camera manual to be sure you know how close is close enough!

Getting Closer

If you want to get a closer view, you have a couple of options. You can use a close-up filter or lens, available with some cameras, that goes over the camera's lens to magnify your subject, or you can move to the camera's minimum focusing distance to shoot the image. Then you can crop the picture digitally on the computer. However, this will result in a loss in quality since you'll need to enlarge the image (see page 28-29 for more information).

GETTING GOOD COLOR

To get in close to small subjects, use a close-up filter or lens on your camera.

Good color starts with a well-exposed picture, whether you're using a digital or conventional film camera. If exposure is bad, your pictures could be too light, too dark, or have weak colors. Shooting in a sunnier location or using flash adds more light to the exposure with either type of camera (conventional or digital).

Of course it's best to start with a well-exposed photo, but color problems can be improved to some extent with simple picture-enhancement programs once you get your picture into the computer.

Flash Options

If your camera's flash is automatic, it will fire whenever the camera *thinks* you need more light. More-advanced flash functions (some automatic and some user-selectable) available on some cameras are red-eye reduction, force flash or flash-on, fill flash, night flash, and flash-off.

If your subject is backlit, you may have the option of using force flash, which causes the flash to fire even if the camera doesn't think it needs it. This will result in a properly exposed subject instead of a silhouette.

Sunny situations can easily create harsh shadows under a subject's eyes, nose, and chin—creating an unpleasant expression or appearance. Fill flash can be used to add a little bit of light from the flash to fill in the shadows, making them less harsh and adding a nice catchlight in the subject's eyes.

If you see an interesting scene, take a photograph, even if you're not sure how it will turn out. The results can be stunning.

Flash-off lets you take long exposures at night without flash, enabling you to get great pictures of neon signs or city lights. Unlike flash-off, night flash mode combines a long exposure (to record ambient background or room lighting) with a subject in the foreground illuminated by flash.

Experiment

There is no better way to learn to take better pictures than to use your camera and study what comes out (or doesn't come out). The great news for digital camera users is that "film" is free. If the picture is bad, a new one can be recorded over it. If it's good, it can be saved to the computer or transferred to a disk, and new pictures can be recorded over the old ones.

Fill the frame. Get in close to your subject or use the camera's telephoto lens setting.

COMPOSITIONAL HINTS

In the next few paragraphs, I'll outline some of the guidelines for good composition. Most are true for any picture, others are specific to the types of pictures commonly used in digital applications.

Fill 'Er Up

As you look through your camera's viewfinder, think of how you plan to use the picture you are making. A full-frame picture of someone might be suited to a family newsletter or a postcard on the Internet. Since you want to show as much about the person as you can in a small picture, "spend" most of your available pixels on the person and not on the background. Don't hesitate to move in close or use the telephoto lens option found on some cameras.

The Big View

On the flip side, good composition in general photography sometimes means stepping back or zooming wide and showing the background as well. In travel photography, for example, a portrait of your family in front of a significant monument is a much more effective remembrance than just a close-up of their faces that could have been taken anywhere.

If you do decide on a wider view, you shouldn't necessarily put the subject dead center in the picture. Some of the best-composed pictures have off-centered subjects. But remember to use the focus-lock option, since almost all point-and-shoot cameras have center-oriented focusing systems.

Fill the frame with multiple planes of information. Placing a subject in the foreground of an interesting landmark adds to the atmosphere and improves the composition.

The Guillotine

Did you inadvertently cut off the heads of your subjects with a point-and-shoot camera? If you were standing close to your subjects, you probably saw their heads in the frame, but parallax was a problem. This phenomenon occurs because the lens you're looking through is not the picture-taking lens, but rather a close approximation of

Instead of putting your subject right in the middle of your photograph, put it off to the side and include more of the scene.

the view the actual taking lens will see. These two lenses see slightly different views, especially when shooting at close range. Parallax lines are usually indicated in the viewfinder if this is a problem. This also explains how your fingers or the camera strap can accidentally appear in your picture. The scene through the viewfinder might look perfect, even when your finger is completely covering the lens!

Avoiding this problem is just a matter of practicing and getting used to the camera you are using. Read the instruction manual and hold the camera the way the manufacturer advises. The old saying "practice makes perfect" was never more true than in photography, no matter what type of camera you use.

Photographing a subject in motion is always difficult, but parallax with point-and-shoot cameras can add to the problem. The view you see in the viewfinder is not always exactly what is recorded!

How'd That Get There?

When you're taking a picture, it's natural to focus your attention on the subject. Our brain is great at filtering out and ignoring distractions, but the camera does not discriminate. When you get your pictures back, you might notice a telephone pole "growing" out of your subject's head, trash at her feet, or a hopeless clutter of distracting elements in front and in back of your subject.

Take a second to decide if shooting from another position will result in a better picture. If you have no choice, take the picture anyway. A little digital magic can correct the problem later.

Shooting at your subject's eye level offers insight into the subject's world.

Eye Level

It's generally best to take portraits at the subject's eye level—whether the subject is tall or short, an adult or child, or even a pet. That means crouching down to photograph children, standing on a step to photograph a basketball player, or lying on the floor to photograph your cat.

Recruit a friend or family member to help out if your pet is wiggly or uncooperative. They can restrain, comfort, or distract the animal while you take the picture. And remember, with digital enhancement software you can make a leash or treat that was used to get your subject to sit still disappear through the magic of retouching.

Taking Great Pet Pictures

Pictures of a pet eating, sleeping, and playing all become part of your picture library. Try taking a variety of pictures using simple backgrounds so that the emphasis is on the pet.

The quickest way to improve your pet pictures is to shoot from their eye level. That usually means kneeling on the floor or raising them up to a level that is comfortable for you. Not only is the resulting portrait more complimentary to your beloved pet, but the picture will be more intimate.

Pictures of your pets can be straight forward or lovely and abstract.

Vertical vs. Horizontal?

Don't forget that you can take vertical pictures by turning the camera sideways. You can always crop a horizontal picture to make it look vertical, but the quality will be better if you shoot it as a vertical originally. Cropping requires enlarging the entire image to produce a comparably sized vertical print, and enlarging always results in a reduction in image quality. It is best to crop as much as possible when composing the picture in the camera's viewfinder and make only minor cropping adjustments later. (See pages 28-29.)

Photograph your subject at eye level for a more pleasing portrait.

Compositional Checklist

Compositional expertise comes from training, practice, and artistic sense. If you ask yourself the following questions before snapping the picture, you will probably improve your results:

- Am I too close? Is parallax a problem?
- Do I want to zoom in on my subject's face or show some of the background?
- Where is my subject in the frame? Is this the most appealing presentation?
- Am I shooting at the subject's eye level?
- Would a horizontal or a vertical format look best?
- Should I use flash?
- Are there shadows on my subject's face? Do I need fill flash?

7 Family Fun with Digital Photography

Digital photography is a terrific creative activity for children.

Digital photography can be a great activity that the whole family can share. Because many computer programs and digital cameras are simple to use, even young children can participate. It is not only a great activity for the family to enjoy together, but it's an excellent tool for fostering creativity and teaching children future scholastic and business skills—all while having fun!

Encourage your children to get involved. If you have ever seen pictures that are made by small children, it's evident that their perspective is completely different from an older sibling's. By making the digital camera available to every family member, there will be a wider variety of pictures to choose from in building your family history.

A little creativity will turn picture-taking and digital photography into a family activity that everyone can look forward to. For example, you could have a treasure hunt, making lists of objects or colors that the children have to find or riddles they have to solve using digital photography. Their photos will be proof of their success. Or make it part of the family routine for everyone to contribute a little something each week to the digital scrapbook. Photo comic books are the modern version of putting on a family puppet show. Or you can turn every member of the family into a reporter for the Smith Family Herald and create a periodic newspaper.

SETTING PARAMETERS

If you own a digital camera, encourage your children to experiment and take photographs. Don't hesitate to use it as a recreational and educational tool.

Editing pictures (deciding which ones to keep and which should be "thrown away") is an important part of the educational process. After your children have shot the day's activities with the digital camera, sit down at the computer and review the pictures with them. Ask them to select their ten best pictures, using documentation or aesthetics as criteria. This will help them review what they've created with a discriminating eye, and it will help you, the parent, understand what your children find important!

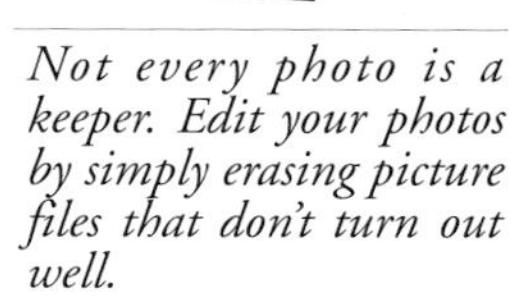

Not every photo is a keeper. Edit your photos by simply erasing picture files that don't turn out well.

And if you're using a conventional camera, remember that film and processing can be expensive. Set up a budget for your youngsters, letting them know how much film they're allowed to shoot each week, and then have them plan their film usage. This simple assignment helps them learn the all-important skills of budgeting, time management, and planning, while giving them the authority and freedom to shoot the pictures they want to shoot.

The following pages cover some of the family- and school-oriented activities that can be done with digital photography.

CALENDARS

All sorts of calendars can be created with software that is available for most computers, and many photofinishing labs offer this service as well. Featuring a single picture for the year or one for every month, a personalized calendar takes on

Why send a store-bought card? Design a photo card especially for the recipient.

special significance and makes a great gift. Older children will enjoy making their own calendars for their school lockers, with pictures of their friends, hobbies, or sports heroes.

Most calendar software allows you to create a calendar either in black and white or color at the touch of a button. Some offer a choice of different date formats. Advanced programs allow you to mark special dates, such as birthdays or holidays, with text and graphics—making it a useful reference for family members.

Either print the calendar on your home printer, or take the image on a disk to a service vendor to have it printed. There you have more options, such as printing on larger paper or very heavy paper stock.

Plan Ahead

Start right now to shoot photos for next year's calendars. Good choices for subjects include anything linked to the seasons (April showers, May flowers, fall leaves, etc.), important holidays (both religious and civic), and family occasions (birthdays, graduations, and anniversaries). Pick pictures that seem appropriate to the month. Don't keep your focus too narrow, though. Digitally enhanced pictures, scenic vacation photos, and scanned artwork by your children are all good choices.

GREETING CARDS AND INVITATIONS

The whole world of personal correspondence is a perfect application for digital photography! Using family pictures, scenic photographs, or anything that can be scanned, you can create greeting cards, postcards, party invitations, announcements, and much, much more. By combining photographs, text, and graphics, you can create unique, personal cards that reflect your feelings of the moment.

There are many software packages that will let you combine your photos with a variety of templates, borders, frames, and clip art. You can create cards of almost any size (within reason!). Once you have designed the card, you can print it out onto heavyweight paper or a blank card specially made to go through a printer.

Postcard software available from several sources allows you to merge a digital picture with text and produce a postcard-sized print that can be sent through the mail. If you make a non-standard-sized postcard, be sure that the finished card meets the post office's size requirements.

Personalize a thank-you card with a photo of the gift in use.

SPECIAL OCCASIONS

The possibilities are endless when it comes to making cards for special occasions. Birth announcements are more meaningful when you include a picture of the newborn. Use a photograph of your new house on a change-of-address card. The same is true for wedding or graduation announcements or thank-you notes.

Party invitations can be fun to make, showing the guest of honor or depicting the party's theme. Think of the creative or funny pictures you could take to illustrate a retirement party or a little boy's baseball-theme birthday party. And the 50th anniversary party invitation just cries out for "then" and "now" pictures.

Make thank-you notes more meaningful by showing the recipient opening the package or enjoying the gift. And on the giving end, adding a picture to a gift tag will personalize a gift. The picture can be of you or the recipient, or it could be a classic symbol, a wedding cake, for instance.

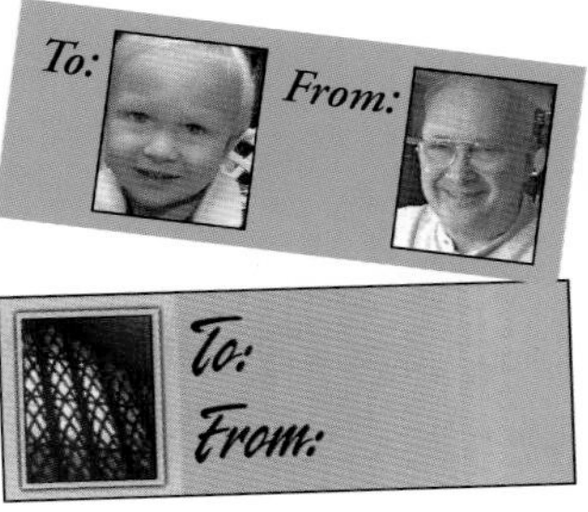

Fonts are fun! Choose a typeface that complements the card, brochure, or cartoon you are creating.

Typefaces

Computers come loaded with many typefaces or fonts from which you can choose (Helvetica, Times, Geneva, etc.). Try several until you find one you like that suits the document you are creating. If you're not satisfied with the fonts supplied, you can purchase others. Some look antique and some look modern, while others resemble handwriting, calligraphy, children's print (with backwards letters and all), or woodcuts. New services can even scan your handwriting and create your own personal handwriting font—if you type an "A," it will look like your hand-printed "A"!

Picking Papers

High-end stationery stores and mail-order companies offer blank or pre-printed papers scored for folding, which can be run through a home printer, making it easy to mass-produce your holiday cards.

And don't forget the envelopes! Most home printers are capable of running envelopes through the manual-feed paper tray. Carry the invitation's or card's theme onto the envelope by printing a small photo by the return address or on the back flap. Make certain you run the envelope through the printer with the flap closed, so if it's moist from humidity, it won't gum up your printer.

STORYBOOKS

Scrapbooks and picture albums tend to be filled with individual vignettes from important moments in our lives. But what about when you want to tell a more complete story? Storybooks created about special events are a great heirloom, and putting them together can be a fun family activity. The idea is to take a group of pictures that when viewed in sequence tell a whole story—whether that story is fictional or real.

Plan, from Start to Finish

Combine photos to cast your friends and family in fictional adventures.

Planning is the key to success here. For example, to commemorate Mother's Day, Dad, Jack, and Jill could take the following pictures to make a terrific storybook:

- Dad, Jack, and Jill having a secret planning meeting in the tree house.
- Jill making a finger-painted Mother's Day card (and a mess).
- Jack making a huge paper-mâché basket (and a mess).
- Dad, Jack, and Jill shopping for gifts to put in the basket.
- Pictures of Jack and Jill holding up silly gift suggestions and real suggestions.
- Dad holding up an empty wallet.
- Jack and Jill pushing a shopping cart with lots of food at the grocery store.
- All three making breakfast.
- Mom with breakfast in bed getting hugs from Jack and Jill.

Later, these photographs can be matched with text, captions, or colorful borders and then printed out and bound inexpensively at a copy center (or professionally by a bookbinder).

Stories and Comic Books

Likewise, you and your kids can create fictional books. Think of them as comic books, making sure that each picture advances the story. Add captions or create dialogue balloons for each picture.

First come up with the story idea and then make out a list of pictures you need. Younger children will probably want to recreate their favorite fairy tales or stories about their television or movie heroes. Older ones will enjoy creating original tales that relate to their lives.

Use costumes, add props, and go on location to shoot pictures, or digitally combine photos to put your characters on horseback, in a castle, or wherever the story takes them. Enlist friends and neighbors as supporting actors and actresses. It's a terrific weekend project that the whole family can get involved in.

STICKER MADNESS

Children love stickers. So why not create your own? Stationery and office supply stores sell adhesive-backed paper that can be used with your home printer. They come in standard sizes pre-cut for address labels or as whole sheets (8-1/2 x 11") that you can later cut into your own shapes. You can get these stickers in clear, white, or fluorescent colors. Some companies also sell star or emblem shapes in gold or silver foil. With these products, your family can combine pictures with text to create unique and personal stickers. The possibilities are endless:

Print on adhesive-backed paper to make bookplates, address labels, and other colorful stickers.

- Bumper stickers
- Address labels
- Stickers for bikes or toys
- Stickers for school notebooks
- Stickers for rewards or encouragement from teachers or parents
- Attention-grabbing notices or highlight stickers for a calendar
- Emergency phone number stickers for the phone or phone book cover
- Stickers that kids design to use on letters or to trade with friends

If you are using an ink jet printer, remember that most of the inks are water-soluble. If the stickers are for outdoor use, spray them with a clear laminate (available from an art supply store) before attaching them.

Pets and Animals

In most families, pets are just like any other family member and deserve their own collection of pictures. Cute pet pictures, digitally sent to family members away from home or to friends who have visited your home, can be a meaningful addition to your family's communication.

With a digital camera, you can be extravagant with the number of pictures you take, picking only the best ones to keep in your pet photo library. Or select pictures from conventional prints or slides and have them scanned or converted to disk or KODAK PHOTO CD formats.

INSTANT ART

Many software programs can transform a photograph into a picture that looks as if it were made using another medium, such as charcoal, pastels, watercolor, or oils. This can often be done with a single keystroke command that changes the texture of the picture to look like one of these painting media. Or you can use more advanced programs to select electronic "paint brushes" of different sizes and types. These can be "dipped" into colors for you to then paint over your pictures. Eraser tools work in a similar fashion, but they lighten or erase the picture wherever they are applied.

Use image-enhancement software to make a photograph look like a painting or drawing.

The fun of these programs is in playing with the different effects. The effects react differently with black-and-white and color pictures or with different subject matter. Don't be afraid to be bold since the picture can always be returned to its original form at the touch of a button. Once you find an effect you like, save the picture under a new name.

Still-Life Photography

As any trip to a museum will prove, still-life paintings and photographs have been a popular subject with artists for centuries. For artistic expression, you too may wish to photograph both extraordinary and commonplace things in your house, office, or neighborhood.

A good way to start is to take a sentimental object and place it in a picturesque setting. Then one by one add other objects in the same way you might arrange flowers in a vase (move one flower to the side, another to the front, and then trim yet another until the arrangement looks perfect). Shift the objects around until everything looks nice together.

When composing the picture, look at the objects in relation to the background. Intermix colors so they complement or play off one another. And remember that the best composition for an artistic picture does not necessarily require that the main subject be in the center. Try composing the picture with it off to one side.

Lighting is important as well. You may choose to turn your flash off and place these objects near a window to take advantage of the ambient light. If the sun streams in, you can achieve a nice interplay of shadow and highlights. And if the window faces north or it's an overcast day, the light will be pleasingly soft.

Once you've taken the picture with either a digital or a conventional camera, the digitized print or negative can be loaded from the floppy disk or KODAK PHOTO CD Disc onto your computer and used as a base to further explore your creativity using paint or drawing photo-enhancement software (see Chapter 5).

If you're short on ideas, browse through art books on painting and photography. Look closely at how the masters used lighting and where the objects are placed in the picture. For practice, you can duplicate their setups.

Put your digital photo into a frame or create a frame using image-enhancement software.

Framing Your Art

After you've shot or enhanced a digital image, you may want to enlarge it for framing. The quality of your result will be affected by how high the image's resolution is and what output device is used to print it (see Chapter 4 for details). If you're not sure how well your digital file will look enlarged, consult the experts at a service bureau and ask to see samples output by different types of printers.

Now for the frame. You have a couple of options. One is to place your picture within a digitally created border in the same fashion you would combine two photographs. Frames are available in many graphics programs, or you can purchase them as clip art (readily available, digitized artwork that you buy the rights to use). Or you can frame it conventionally with mat board and a frame from a photo shop or frame store.

8 Preserving History

Digital imaging and computers offer new ways to record and preserve history. A digital scrapbook can be a source of great creativity and family interaction. Pictures can be integrated into the text, and text can be added to pictures. Memorabilia, such as ticket stubs, invitations, or flowers can be digitized as well.

Scrapbooks and Albums

The perfect time to start a digital family scrapbook is from the time you first acquire the equipment, keeping and storing pictures and mementos along with stories, dates, times, and places of memorable events. But no matter when you start, it's not too late! The beauty of the computer age is that, unlike a paper scrapbook, you can add "pages" anywhere in the sequence without pulling the whole thing apart or having to search for compatible refill pages. Start now, and gradually work your way backwards. By the time the holidays hit, you'll probably have the whole family history out of the shoe box and onto the computer (or printed out in a nice, neat booklet).

Family Tradition

If you're serious about archiving your family's life (and believe me, it's a document that is certain to become a family heirloom), then you should consider bringing the whole family in on the project. For example, you can make it a habit to gather everyone around the computer for ten minutes every Sunday night, before or after dinner. Ask everyone to contribute a sentence, a digital picture, or an item to be scanned (if you have a home scanner). The words can be a simple synopsis of a highlight in their week or a new joke they learned at school. The visuals could be a photograph, a piece of artwork, a ticket stub, or even the high-score screen grabbed off the video game with a video image-capture device. The point is that it's their contribution, and it will reflect their personality when you look back on it later.

Include candid photos and family portraits in your scrapbook. Photos like these are sure to bring back nostalgic memories when viewed along with scanned images of ticket stubs to a memorable event or a child's artwork.

Bound to Be an Heirloom

With this scrapbook in hand at major holidays, you'll be able to look back at the events of the previous months or years and enjoy reminiscing together about your family's growth. Having this document printed out onto special paper or even bound into a book would be a great present to give to family members. You can have it covered inexpensively at a copy shop, or you can go all the way and take it to a bookbinder. Emboss the cover in gold letters with your family's name. What grandparent wouldn't love that as a gift?

No Negatives?

An archive, family album, or shoe box in the closet may be filled with pictures for which there are no negatives. Any picture can be digitized with a home scanner or by taking it to a service bureau or photo laboratory that offers scanning services. Either way, you'll end up with a digitized file that is transferable to your computer through a floppy disk or KODAK PHOTO CD Disc. You can also repair photos damaged from fading, tears, creases, or stains. Digitizing these pictures by scanning them enables you to do this with simple retouching programs.

Digitally retouch photos to remove glare and other distracting elements.

You might want to share these pictures by making digital copies. These picture files can then be printed at home or at a service bureau, or they can be sent over the Internet as e-mail.

Retouching Hint

For removing scratches or making other repairs, enlarge the digital image as much as possible so that you can easily see what you are doing. Even the most unsteady hand can do an adequate job when working on a greatly enlarged view of the image.

Retouching Options

Enhancement, retouching, or damage correction can be done by a service bureau or on your home personal computer using photo-enhancement software. Scratches can be eliminated, dirt or stains removed, and in general the image can be preserved (albeit in a new form). In addition, titles can be placed on pictures so that names of people and locations can be recalled in the future (see Chapter 5 for more details). Photos can also be combined as interesting montages or collages.

A Note of Caution about Copyright

It's important to know a little bit about copyright laws if you are working with pictures that you did not take. If the picture is protected by copyright, it is illegal for you to reproduce it or even have it scanned. For example, with a professional portrait, you only own the print that you bought from the photographer, not the right to reproduce it. You must have the photographer's permission to copy the photograph. In fact, a photo lab or service bureau that reprints, copies, or scans a photograph that has copyright protection (frequently stamped on the back) is subject to fines unless they have the photographer's written consent.

DEAR DIARY...

Diaries have always served as wonderful memory-keepers for children and a great outlet for personal expression. The exciting times at school and after school can be quickly recorded in words, but now digital pictures add a whole new dimension. Of course, adults keep diaries as well, but we try to fool ourselves by calling them "journals" or "memoirs"!

Most new word processing programs allow you to add photographs to text documents quickly and easily. After teaching your kids how to do this with your particular software program (or more likely, after they teach you!), you will all be ready to go.

Why Don't I Own My Wedding Pictures?

Most professional wedding photographers charge comparatively very little to shoot your wedding, making most of their money by selling prints of the photographs to you and your family. It works out well for the bride and groom, because they don't have to buy many pictures unless they are pleased with the results—giving the photographer plenty of incentive to do a great job. If they were to buy one print and then make dozens of their own copies for friends and family, they'd be cheating the photographer out of his or her hard-earned living, and they'd be breaking the law. This is because in most cases the photographer owns the copyright to the pictures, and you own only the prints that you buy.

Lock and Key

A diary is something very personal and usually meant for the writer's eyes only. Just like the old lock-and-key diaries, you can use inexpensive security software to "lock" private digital files or documents with passwords or codes. Or, the diary can simply be saved to a disk (rather than on the computer's hard drive), which can then be stored in a safe, private place. Be sure to make a backup disk or file away a hard copy in case of a computer "crash" or disk failure.

HOMETOWN HISTORIAN

Whether it's for your own personal archive, for the local historical society, or just to share with friends and relatives, your city or hometown can be a great subject to photograph. The photos can be captured with a digital camera or you can turn your best conventional prints into digital files.

Better Directions

If you have friends or family visiting from out of town, you can get them excited about the trip and keep them from getting lost with digital pictures. A picture of your house, driving directions, and a map put together in collage form will do the trick. Photographs of exit signs and landmarks will make your instructions easier to follow. Adding the tourist sites or points of interest will sweeten the package. Every time you need to give directions to your house, just print out a copy of the map or send it via e-mail.

Cross Brink Road

Elm Drive

Turn RIGHT on Elm Drive
(There is a BARN on corner)

In a city or a rural setting, there are plenty of great picture opportunities surrounding you, such as sunsets, skylines, local signs and attractions, interesting architecture, and local gardens. View everyday sights with a fresh eye and try to view some of the subjects as art forms. Don't forget to take close-ups that allow you to see clearly all those things that you walk by every day that you may have taken for granted. Or concentrate on a theme such as doors, mail boxes, fences, or gardens. Play with unusual angles, compositions, shapes, lines, and colors.

Photograph all those sights and attractions that make your hometown special.

Tell the story of your neighborhood through taking pictures of the people and the places. And be sure to include text comments in the digital file so that in later years you will be able to identify the people and the places in the photos.

NEWSLETTERS

Newsletters are a fun and effective way to get information out to all your relatives and friends. And thanks to computers, each newsletter can have personal touches added for the recipient. Don't just send many copies of the exact same letter.

Start by writing a letter that recounts all the information and events you want to share with everyone. Before printing it however, personalize each copy for the individual it's going to (thanking Grandma for the wonderful holiday gifts or adding a photo of your house and a map for Aunt Betty's upcoming visit).

The newsletter could be a family project as well, giving story assignments to every member of the family (Mom and Dad included!). Each person has to research, write, and photograph the story.

Smith Family Rides in the Tour de Cure

by Rochelle Smith

Avid bicyclists Jeff, John, and Mindy Smith rode with members of their cycling club to raise money for a good cause—the MS Tour de Cure.

Fancy Graphics

Your newsletter can look just like a handwritten letter—with customized handwriting fonts. Or you can make it look like a professional newsletter or newspaper by dividing the text into columns and adding headlines and photographs. Even simple word processing programs usually have these capabilities.

Shooting Hints

- Don't be afraid to make pictures on a cloudy day, often the light is soft and flattering.
- Use close-up attachments to show details of doorways or flowers.
- Fill the viewfinder of your camera with important picture elements.
- Include identifiable features like statues, school facades, or other landmarks.

School Days 9

Conventional, film-based cameras are often used in schools to help students capture, study, support, and remember school events and experiences. This practice still continues, but with the advent of digital cameras, taking pictures in school situations becomes a more dynamic and exciting opportunity. Students and teachers can use the technology to combine text with pictures in the computer for reports or to create classroom computer "bulletin boards."

Our Class Trip to the Zoo...
Take photos on field trips for the students to use in reports, stories, or other assignments.

HELP TEACHERS TO THINK "DIGITALLY"

If you're active in your community or the local PTA, you can suggest that teachers consider using digital cameras in your school system. The big benefit is that after the initial cost outlay, there are no additional film or processing expenditures to budget for, resulting in a large cost savings for the school district over the years.

Think about it. Having equipment to support digital photography in the schools is like purchasing a candy store with an unlimited supply of candy. Digital pictures, particularly those made by digital cameras, are stored in devices that can be used over and over again. Pictures are transferred to a computer, where they can be viewed instantly without waiting (or paying) for processing. They can then be integrated into a report, presentation, or anywhere that the teacher or student decides a picture could be used.

The exciting possibilities of using pictures in everyday school reports or homework assignments will not take away from developing language skills,

but will allow students to correlate their visual and writing skills. And most of the projects listed in this book can be done in the classroom as well as at home.

FIELD TRIPS

School field trips are tremendous opportunities for students to take digital pictures. If a written report is required, photographic documentation adds a whole new dimension to the experience.

Sit down with the students and talk about the upcoming field trip. Discuss how the day might go and point out some potential shooting opportunities. Give them each an assignment that will determine the theme of their particular photo essay or report. In general, a broad-based report might include: 1) getting to the destination; 2) people they encountered, for example the tour guide or staff members; 3) points of interest, such as monuments or artifacts; and 4) pictures of classmates combined with their comments.

One thing to remember is that some museums and other public buildings do not permit the use of flash photography. Make sure your students know how to turn the flash off and how to hold the camera extra steady if they need to take a picture in a dark location where flash is forbidden.

Dear Yuri,
This is a picture of me in my baseball uniform. Do you play baseball in Russia?...

PEN PALS

Having pen pals is a way for students throughout the world to meet each other and share their cultures—while practicing their writing and foreign language skills. It gives each party interesting insights into the life of the other, but the process of exchanging letters is long and slow. Now e-mail (electronic mail) makes communication faster. Pen pals can even communicate in real time through the Internet. Today a student in Ashland,

Ohio, can exchange both words and pictures with his or her electronic pen pals in Vladivostok, Russia, or Tokyo, Japan.

Children can add photos to descriptions of school events and field trips to create a personal yearbook.

Personal Yearbook

A great project for a child is to create his or her own school yearbook. It can be thought of as a scrapbook with a theme, all occurring within the confines of one year. Encourage your child to combine photographs they have shot with school pictures, varsity letters, and other memorabilia. (Remember that drawings, pictures, and other flat objects can all be scanned.)

If your child's friends want to get involved, it can be a terrific group project—with everyone contributing words and images. When they're all done, you can have copies printed and bound at a copy shop.

Don't forget to remind the kids to take fun pictures of some of the crazy things that happen at recess or sporting events! If they can't get a picture, they can describe the event in words. And when adding captions to photographs encourage them to be as detailed as possible—it might seem obvious now, but years from now the names and events will fade from memory. They might even tell some of the funny (or serious) stories that go along with the pictures or interview friends about the event that is taking place.

Simple Cameras

The newest digital cameras are simple point-and-shoot cameras that can be used by all age groups. A preschooler can enjoy a picture of a friend, pet, or playground scene. The high school or university student can add digital pictures to school reports or papers to make them come alive and to back up the written word. New word processing programs are now so easy that pictures can often be added to a document with one command—so once your kids

Improve your game. Review photos taken with a digital camera as soon as you get home to your computer.

can read and write, they can combine pictures and words on the computer!

SPORTS AND HOBBIES

Sports programs play a major part in many young people's lives throughout their school years. Digital pictures are useful when compiling a scrapbook, but they can also be used as a training record. By taking pictures with a digital camera (or grabbing pictures off a high-speed video), your young sports hero can observe his or her technique and form, and with the coach's help, learn to improve it. Your child's coach would probably be delighted if you offered your services to photograph the whole team for training purposes. You can then use these same pictures to make baseball cards of each player by using techniques described in Chapter 5 to combine the athlete's picture with the team logo, player's name, and vital statistics.

The field or court are not the only places you'll find great sports pictures. Take pictures of benched players, coaching huddles, cheerleaders, coaches, fans, and the team mascot. They also tell the story of the event.

Use digital photos to check your stance and swing.

Shooting Sports

If you want to analyze a specific athletic maneuver, like a golf swing, plan the picture carefully. Have the player stand in front of a simple background devoid of clutter. Ask them to practice the action a few times, so you get the feel for the rhythm of the motion and can predict when to best shoot the height of action.

If sequence shooting is desired, you'll probably need to use a conventional camera with a high-speed motor drive, since most entry-level digital cameras have about a 5-second recycle time. Better yet, you can use a video camcorder with a high-speed shutter capability, such as 1/10,000 second. Then capture still pictures at consecutive split-second intervals with frame-grabbing hardware and software to study the entire arc of the golf or baseball swing.

INTERNET FUN

The Internet has been around for years, but only recently has it become easily accessible to anyone with a computer and a modem. Many large corporations and schools offer employees and students unlimited access—a big perk if you find "Net surfing" a useful research or entertainment tool.

While nobody owns the Internet, you do need to "access" it—and the easiest way to do this is to subscribe to an Internet service (see page 7 for more information about the Internet). Internet providers are available in almost every part of the world to sell access to the Internet and allow the free exchange of mail and messages. National services like America Online® or CompuServe® have made it simple, supplying you with free software to use and charging an access fee or per-hour usage fees. Plus local

In the News

Another great project for a parent, teacher, or coach to do with their children or students is to work together in writing a "newspaper" story about the game. Here's one writing assignment that even the most reticent child or student will love to complete. See page 57 for hints on how to do this.

If they're especially young or are having trouble getting started with the writing, give them the headline and the first few sentences. For example, "It was a close call, but the Livonia Comets pulled together to come up with an impressive win over their long-time rivals, the Royal Oak Racers. It all started with a home run by..."

COMETS WIN FOUR STRAIGHT

by Robbie Smith

LIVONIA,MI--The Livonia Comets have won four straight games, putting them in first place of the Division A/Under-12 league. Led by star pitcher Katie Smith, the Comets scored a total of 9 runs in the series, allowing only 2 runs by the opposition....

phone companies and others are offering competitive local services for "hooking in." And don't forget cable TV—the next big Internet wave will be connection through your TV, no computer required! (Setup boxes with wireless keyboards may be the next addition to the home entertainment center.)

When the kids do something cute, send a digital picture instantly to every family member.

E-Mail

Electronic mail, or e-mail, is one of the big perks of being on the Internet. When you sign onto a service, you get an "address," usually one that you can pick yourself, based on your name or a hobby. You can then correspond with anyone else on the Net.

And you can do more than just send messages. You can attach picture files, graphics, and virtually any other digital file. They are sent quickly, and it's covered in your access fee and the cost of using local phone service.

Sending Electronic Pictures

You'll want to send electronic pictures for all the same reasons you send conventional photographic prints—keeping in touch with family, corresponding with pen pals, sending birth announcements, and so on. However, there are advantages to sending and receiving photographs digitally through e-mail, such as instant delivery and the savings incurred by not having to make many prints.

The least complicated way to send a picture through electronic mail is to send it as a file attached to an e-mail document. Or you can create a document using software that allows you to integrate pictures into the text and then send the document via e-mail. However, the receiver must also have the software used to create the document.

Don't wait for a catalog to come in the mail. Ask a company to e-mail you a photo of a particular product, or visit a company's web site to view and order merchandise.

The Professional Edge 10

In the business environment, the beauty of a digital camera is that it gives you instant results (no more running to the lab and waiting for the prints) and after the initial purchase, it's less expensive than conventional film-based photography (there's no film to buy or processing to pay for). However, if you don't have a digital camera, your business can still take advantage of these benefits with scanned photographs delivered on floppy disk or on a KODAK PHOTO CD Disc, allowing you to combine pictures with text in all of your business documents.

From wine cellars to warehouses, digital cameras are ideal for documenting your property, products, and inventory.

RÉSUMÉ PICTURES

There's no better way to let a prospective employer know you're on the cutting edge of technology than by including your picture on your résumé or cover letter. Not only does the computer let you tailor each letter and résumé to the exact position you're applying for, but you can customize your photo as well. You can photograph yourself in a business suit or dressed in fashionable clothes, depending on the business environment of the prospective employer. And, if special skills are required for the job, your picture can show you in action.

Since this picture will be the first impression an employer will have of you, make certain it is top quality and shows you in a favorable light. You may want to have a professional photographer take the picture in a studio. But be certain to explain to the photographer what the photo is intended to be used for—since certain poses would not be appropriate for a résumé. In this photo you'd want to exude confidence and business savvy. Be sure to ask family and friends which picture best reflects those qualities and why, since it's sometimes very hard to be objective when looking at pictures of yourself.

Performers can show themselves in action on business cards, résumés, and brochures.

LOGOS, LETTERHEAD, AND CARDS

One of the first steps in starting your own business is to create business documents and sales tools that have a professional look. Digital photography gives you a whole new way to create logos, letterhead, business cards, and more.

You can include a portrait of yourself, a picture of your storefront, or an image that represents your products or services. Combine this photograph with your company name and other pertinent information, and you're ready to go.

You can purchase color-coordinated stationery on which your logo and address can be printed with your home printer. Sheets perforated for making business cards can be run through your printer at a moment's notice. Just print them, break them apart, and start passing them out.

The most important thing to remember is consistency. You want every document that leaves your office to have the same look, for example, through the logo and the typeface you use. That way, not only will your company project a more professional image, but your documents and marketing materials will be easily recognized by your clients and be more effective.

Plenty of books on logos and business designs have been published to help you get started. Or you can hire a graphic designer to create a graphic identity for you and deliver it as a digital file that you can use on your stationery, brochures, marketing pieces, invoices, business cards, and e-mail.

PICTURE PHONE BOOK

Do you have trouble keeping track of clients or putting names to faces? You can create a picture phone book by inserting a picture of your client into your computer phone files. A quick digital snapshot or a scanned clipping from a brochure or sales piece will do the trick.

If you use a card-style indexing system, you can purchase sheets of perforated cards. Simply print the names, addresses, phone numbers, and photos in the proper places on the paper, tear the cards apart, and you have an impressive address system.

ADVERTISEMENTS AND BROCHURES

With a digital picture and text, you can create any number of advertisements, brochures, and promotional pieces. The easiest method is to use a word processing program that enables you to insert photographs. But advanced graphics layout programs, which are more expensive and require more time to learn, will allow you to replicate virtually any type of advertisement you'll see in magazines, newspapers, and direct-mail pieces.

Marketing Brochures and Pamphlets

To create a simple brochure, design the page sideways (landscape mode) and set it up for a three-column format. In this way, an 8-1⁄2 x 11-inch sheet of paper can be tri-folded and placed in a No. 10 envelope. It can get a little tricky if you're making a folding brochure, because the text on the left column of the first page might not be on the front of the brochure once it's folded. More likely, either the right- or left-hand panel on the back will be on the front. To figure this out, simply take a piece of blank paper, fold it, and then sketch out where the pictures,

Using a simple Z-fold design makes it easier to lay out a brochure.

A picture is worth a thousand words. A digital photo can be easily inserted into any layout created with a desktop publishing program.

headlines, and text should be. Then unfold it, and create your brochure using this mock-up as a guide.

Stock Forms and Papers

You can tell how far desktop publishing has come by the large number of paper products available for desktop printers. You can purchase card stock or heavy-weight papers that are scored so that your brochures can be folded neatly. Some even come perforated with index filing cards that clients can detach and save for future reference. Others come pre-printed with four-color graphics over which you print your type and black-and-white pictures. The end result is a brochure or sales piece that looks like it was printed professionally.

You can even buy 11 x 17-inch newsletter paper with four-color designs and blank boxes for individual stories. Just write copy to fit these spaces, print it, fold it in half, and presto, you have a professional-looking four-page newsletter. And of course, matching envelopes and stationery are available as well.

RE: PARKING
Four parking spaces in the North Street lot have been reserved for our neighbors. Please observe the signs.

Include a photo with your memo or inter-office e-mail to get your message across.

MEMOS AND STATUS REPORTS

Establish yourself as an effective communicator by dressing up your memos, status reports, and other internal documents with pictures. You'll be amazed how much easier it is to communicate with staff or clients when written or verbal information is supported by photos.

For example, if you're writing a memo about the security hazard caused by a broken window, include a photograph! Not only will your memo be noticed and read first, but the picture will get the point across better than a page of text could.

Likewise, imagine the increased impact of a status report that describes the successful implementation of a new assembly-line process and shows a picture to back up the written word.

CERTIFICATES

Honor your employees, clients, friends, and family with certificates of recognition. Preprinted certificate forms are available, or you can create your own using hand-drawn or clip art frames. Remember that a certificate can be much more than simply words on paper. Using a picture of a person's face, a product, or a relevant symbol will make it more unique and rewarding.

You can have fun with the typeface, picking a bold, easy-to-read font, or an ornate Old English style. Calligraphy fonts offer a traditional flair. To add class, you can affix a ribbon with sealing wax or foil stickers. Products are also available that will add a metallic finish to a laser-printed document. The foil adheres only to the toner so a word or graphic can be transformed from black into shiny gold. Traditional choices for presentation include simple folders or envelopes, or a more elaborate frame or wooden plaque.

INVENTORY AND QUICK RESPONSE

Whether you're in the antiques, real estate, or auto parts business, digital photography can be an invaluable tool to let your customers see what you have in stock.

For example, an antiques dealer can now show a collector a perfect Edwardian bureau by quickly photographing it with a digital camera, digitizing a conventional print on a home scanner, or having the picture transferred to a KODAK PHOTO CD Disc. The picture file, photo CD, or printed copy can be sent to a prospective customer via e-mail, fax, or through the postal service!

Customers can see your products immediately if you send them a digital photo via e-mail.

Likewise, real estate agents can update their listings with pictures, placing them digitally next to a

Real estate agents can print out copies of a house's sell sheet complete with a picture whenever needed.

written description of the house. The digital file can then be printed out as needed—no more sorting through negatives to have photographs reprinted. When the house sells, the picture can be erased. This is a convenient and inexpensive way to maintain a listing gallery.

INSURANCE PURPOSES

Digital imaging offers convenient documentation and storage of property records for insurance purposes. Photograph your valuables and have the images put onto a photo CD. A single disk holds up to 100 images. As an added measure, scan the purchase receipts and save them to a floppy disk. Advance preparation will save time and confusion if you are ever faced with fire, flood, theft, or other losses. Everything you need will be in one compact, convenient file. Just be certain to store back-up copies of these pictures off-site in a secure place. (You wouldn't want your pictures to be stored on the hard drive if the computer is stolen or your disks to be burned along with the building.)

The insurance business is a growing field for digital photography. Damage photos taken with a digital camera can be viewed immediately by an adjuster in the field and then transmitted via modem to the company headquarters.

MARKETING WITH THE WEB

The Internet's commercial sector, the World Wide Web, is becoming an international phenomenon (see page 7 for more information). Large and small companies are now including the "http" web site addresses on their business cards, stationery, advertisements, and brochures. The Web is made up of "home pages" or "web sites" for businesses and private individuals. These pages can be linked automatically with other web sites.

Web sites are basically business advertisements, but they often include entertaining, useful, or educational information as well. Product photos can be taken with a digital camera, downloaded directly onto a computer, and integrated into a business's web site. For example, a sporting goods store's web site might provide up-to-date information of the basketball draft to lure customers into visiting their store and hopefully looking at the new products they have to offer. Constantly updating a web site is important to draw people back.

Use your digital camera to make a record of your belongings for insurance purposes.

Software is available to help you create your own web site, should you want to take advantage of the countless marketing opportunities made available by the Internet. First investigate the Web thoroughly and see how other businesses' web sites are designed. Yours should be as easy to access and comprehend as your best marketing brochure. And if you have doubts about your creative abilities, don't worry, there are thousands of individuals and companies who offer web services, including developing, monitoring, and updating your web site for you.

Showcase Your Products on the Web

When creating your web page, choose photos that showcase your products and convey the character of your business.

Glossary

Aliasing A defect caused by the insufficient digital sampling of a scene when the image is captured or by the low resolution capability of the monitor displaying an image. This term is most often used to refer to the jagged appearance of diagonal or curved lines when viewed on a monitor. (See also Jaggies.)

Analog Information represented in continuous form by an infinite number of values. A conventional photograph is considered to be an analogous item as it has an infinite range of color, shapes, and density. Analog is the opposite of digital. (See Digital.)

Application Software A type of computer program designed to allow the user to perform a specific use, task, or function (such as word processing, budgeting, or playing games).

Artifact Visible or audible extraneous information in a signal that produces a defect in the image or sound.

Bit Abbreviation for Binary Digit. A bit is the smallest unit of data in a computer system. Each bit is represented by a 1 or a 0 in binary code or digitally in a computer by an "on" or "off" electronic pulse.

Bits Per Second (BPS) A measurement of the speed of information transmission. The number of bits of information transmitted in one second.

Byte A sequence of eight adjacent bits operated by the computer as if they were a single unit. The storage capacity of a computer is measured in bytes. 1024 bytes is called a kilobyte (K), and 1024 kilobytes is called a megabyte (MB).

Cathode Ray Tube (CRT) A type of picture tube used in a television set or monitor. Inside this tube, an electron gun generates beams of electrons that illuminate specific phosphors on the screen to produce an image.

CCD (Charge-Coupled Device) A device that converts light into an electronic signal.

CCD Camera A solid-state camera that utilizes a charge-coupled device to digitize acquired images. CCD cameras read pixel brightness serially in a line-by-line scan pattern.

CD-ROM (Compact Disc Read-Only Memory) A CD-ROM disk looks like a music CD. It is an efficient device that stores large quantities of information in read-only format. It can hold up to 600 megabytes of information and is particularly useful for storing graphic images due to their large memory requirements. To "play" a CD-ROM disk, a built-in or peripheral CD-ROM drive is required.

CMYK An abbreviation for Cyan, Magenta, Yellow, blacK. The transparent ink colors used in the four-color printing process. These four ink colors are combined in a dot pattern to create a realistic-looking image. The four color separations required for printing can be produced by most graphics and image-manipulation software.

Color Correction A process of adjusting color values to achieve accuracy in color reproduction. This process can be likened to adjusting the colors on your TV set. Color correction is important because the colors of an image viewed on your monitor are not necessarily the same as those you will see when the image is printed. Therefore, for accurate color output, the monitor must be calibrated or color corrected to match the output of the printer in use.

Color Fringing An image defect in the printed image in which separate layers of colors appear on an area of the image where two colors meet.

Compression A technique used to reduce the size of a data file, thereby reducing the amount of disk space required to store the data file or the time required to send a file. A compressed image must be decompressed to be viewed or used. While compression is advantageous for storing or transmitting an image, it can cause degradation of the image even after it is decompressed.

Data Compression The use of a coding technique to reduce the volume of stored data. (See also Compression.)

Digital Information that is encoded as a series of discrete "on" or "off" electrical pulses based on a binary coding system (1 or 0). The opposite of analog. For instance, a conventional, analog photograph must be broken down into discrete pieces of information (1 or 0) in order for it to be "understood" by a computer. (See Analog.)

Digital Camera A device that interprets images in the form of a series of discrete values (or binary numbers) that can be used by a computer.

Dots Per Inch (DPI) A unit used to describe the resolution of a printer or scanner. The number of units that appear in sequence in one linear inch of the image. (See also Resolution.)

Film Scanner A piece of equipment used to convert color negatives and slides digitally into electronic images.

Hard Copy A computer document that has been printed. It could be a paper copy or a transparency.

Hard Disk Also called a hard drive. A disk drive with high storage capacity. This is usually where the computer's system files, application, and utilities programs are stored. The hard disk's high storage capacity is achieved by utilizing a rigid form of magnetic media and extremely close mechanical tolerances.

Hertz (Hz) The unit of electrical frequency equal to one cycle per second (cps); one kilohertz (KHz) equals 1,000 cps; one megahertz (MHz) equals 1,000,000 cps. (See Megahertz.)

Image Enhancement Changing a digital image so that it is more pleasing to the eye. Photo software programs allow an image to be sharpened or contrast to be increased or decreased, for example.

Ink Jet Printer A non-impact printer that utilizes droplets of ink to create information on a page. As the printhead moves across the surface of the page, it shoots out a stream of tiny, electrostatically charged ink droplets, placing them precisely to form letters or an image.

Jaggies A term used to describe the jagged, or stair-stepped, appearance of diagonal lines in computer-generated, bit-mapped graphic images. Also called aliasing or stair-stepping. (See Aliasing.)

JPEG Abbreviation for Joint Photographic Experts Group. A graphics file format that is a standardized method for compressing and decompressing still-image files. It reduces the size of a file to about 1/20 its original size. JPEG is considered a "lossy" compression format, meaning that some digital information is lost whenever a compression or decompression takes place. (See also Lossless, Lossy.)

Kilobyte (K) 1024 bytes of data. The memory capacity, especially RAM, of a computer device is generally described in terms of "K"s.

Lossless A term used to described a compression program that does not lose image data when a file is compressed or decompressed.

Lossy A term used to described a compression program that loses image data every time a compression or decompression is performed.

Megabyte (MB) 1024 kilobytes (approximately one million bytes).

Megahertz (MHz) One million hertz. A unit of frequency equal to one million cycles per second. Refers to the speed at which a computer's processor operates.

Memory Card An electronic circuit board that stores large amounts of digital data on memory chips. Memory cards can be used in digital cameras, computers, and other consumer electronic products. Also called PC cards or flash cards. (See also PC Card.)

Monitor A TV-like display device that makes the information in a computer or other electronic device visible. Monitors are essentially televisions without tuner or receiver mechanisms.

Output Data that comes out of a computer device; also, a video or audio signal that is emitted from a system.

PC Card Formerly called PCMCIA cards, these are solid-state memory modules that can be plugged into a digital camera or computer. They come in three standard thicknesses (Types I, II, and III) and are made in many varieties. PCMCIA stands for Personal Computer Memory Card International Association. (See also Memory Card.)

Peripheral A piece of equipment that is separate from but connected to a computer (CPU) and controlled by it. For example, keyboards, printers, and scanners are considered computer peripherals.

Pixel Short for picture element. The smallest element in a digital image. A one-bit pixel can display one of two colors, a two-bit pixel can display one of four colors or shades of gray, four bits can display 16 colors or shades of gray, and so forth.

Pixels Per Inch (PPI) The term used to describe the number of units displayed in a linear inch on a computer monitor. The number of pixels per inch that a monitor is capable of determines the monitor's best level of image resolution. (See also Resolution.)

RAM (Random Access Memory) The memory available in the computer for creating, loading, or running programs and for temporarily storing and manipulating data.

Resolution The sharpness or clarity of an image. Resolution is important to monitor viewing and printer output. With monitors, the density and overall quality of the image on the screen is determined by the size and organization of its pixels. Generally, the higher the number of pixels per inch (ppi), the finer the display, but no matter how many pixels the monitor is capable of displaying, the computer must have adequate memory to enable a finely resolved display. With printers, resolution is measured in dots per inch (dpi) and lines per inch (lpi). The more dots that can be printed per inch (horizontally), and the more lines that can be printed per inch (vertically), the better the image resolution.

RGB Red, Green, and Blue. These are the colors that are used to create full-color images in color television sets and computer monitors. RGB images must be converted to CMYK for four-color process printing. (See also CMYK.)

VRAM Video Random Access Memory is used on some video adapters to increase the speed at which an image can be displayed on the screen.

PHOTO CREDITS

Jenni Bidner: Front cover photo (Andrea Zocchi, image manipulation)
Joann Brennan: 5 (top), 8 (center, bottom), 10 (top), 17 (top), 20 (top), 21, 22, 28 (top), 31 (bottom), 56 (top), 65, 69 (bottom)
James DiBella: 4 (bottom), 7 (top), 10 (center), 12 (top), 14
Eastman Kodak Company: 15, 17 (bottom), 34 (top), 41 (top), 42, 43 (top), 49 (top), 52 (top), 60 , 61, 62 (bottom), 71 (bottom)
Keith F. Freeberg, Jr.: 57 (top, bottom)
Alexis Gerard: 18 (top), 27 (bottom), 40 (bottom), 50 (top)
Paul Gilman: 4 (center), 6 (bottom), 11, 13 (fireworks), 16 (top), 19, 20 (bottom), 23, 24, 27 (top), 36 (bottom), 45 (top), 52 (top), 58 (center), 64 (bottom), 66 (top), 69 (top)
James Jarrett: 18 (bottom)
John Larish: 6 (top), 8 (top), 25, 26, 30 (top), 32, 33 (top), 34 (bottom), 37 (top), 38 (bottom), 41 (center, bottom), 43 (bottom), 44 (top), 45 (center), 46, 47, 48, 49 (bottom), 50 (bottom), 51 (bottom), 53 (top), 54, 55, 59, 62 (top), 63, 66 (bottom), 67, 68 (top), 70, 71 (top)
Paul Lee: 5 (bottom), 45 (bottom), 68 (bottom)
David M. Lewis: 9 (top), 12 (bottom), 36 (top), 39 (bottom)
Norma Matley: 4 (top), 16 (bottom), 33 (bottom), 37 (bottom), 39 (top)
Michael J. May: 7 (bottom), 35, 44 (bottom)
Marianna O'Brien: 9 (bottom), 38 (top)
Jeffrey Peters: 57 (center)
David Schoeffler: 28 (bottom), 40 (top), 53 (bottom), 64 (top)
Paul Schulze: 10 (bottom), 40 (center), 51 (top), 56 (center, bottom)
Stephen P. Smith: 13 (castle), 29, 31 (top)
Rodney Thompson: 58 (top, bottom)
Joseph Vivinetto: 19 (illustrations)

Notes